PLANT BASED COOKBOOK 2022

DELICIOUS RECIPES TO INCREASE YOUR ENERGY

RICE AND GRAINS

CHARLES TRUMP

Table of Contents

Introduciton 10

RICE & GRAINS 12

Classic Garlicky Rice 13

Brown Rice with Vegetables and Tofu 15

Basic Amaranth Porridge 17

. Country Cornbread with Spinach 19

Rice Pudding with Currants 21

Millet Porridge with Sultanas 23

Quinoa Porridge with Dried Figs 26

Bread Pudding with Raisins 28

Bulgur Wheat Salad 30

Rye Porridge with Blueberry Topping 32

Coconut Sorghum Porridge 34

Dad's Aromatic Rice 36

Everyday Savory Grits 38

Greek-Style Barley Salad 40

Easy Sweet Maize Meal Porridge 42

Mom's Millet Muffins 44

Ginger Brown Rice 46

Sweet Oatmeal "Grits" 48

Freekeh Bowl with Dried Figs 50

Cornmeal Porridge with Maple Syrup 53

Mediterranean-Style Rice 55

Bulgur Pancakes with a Twist 57

Chocolate Rye Porridge 59

Authentic African Mielie-Meal 61

Teff Porridge with Dried Figs 63

Decadent Bread Pudding with Apricots 66

Chipotle Cilantro Rice 68

Oat Porridge with Almonds 70

Aromatic Millet Bowl 72

Harissa Bulgur Bowl 74

Coconut Quinoa Pudding 77

Cremini Mushroom Risotto 79

Colorful Risotto with Vegetables 81

Amarant Grits with Walnuts 83

Barley Pilaf with Wild Mushrooms 85

Sweet Cornbread Muffins 87

Aromatic Rice Pudding with Dried Figs 90

Potage au Quinoa 92

Sorghum Bowl with Almonds 94

Bulgur Muffins with Raisins.. 96

Old-Fashioned Pilaf.. 98

Freekeh Salad with Za'atar 100

Vegetable Amaranth Soup 102

Polenta with Mushrooms and Chickpeas...................................105

Teff Salad with Avocado and Beans 107

Overnight Oatmeal with Walnuts 109

Carrot Energy Balls 111

Crunchy Sweet Potato Bites..113

Roasted Glazed Baby Carrots 115

Oven-Baked Kale Chips..117

Cheesy Cashew Dip...119

Peppery Hummus Dip 121

Traditional Lebanese Mutabal 124

Indian-Style Roasted Chickpeas 126

Avocado with Tahini Sauce 128

Sweet Potato Tater Tots 130

Roasted Pepper and Tomato Dip..132

Classic Party Mix 134

Olive Oil Garlic Crostini 136

Classic Vegan Meatballs...137

Balsamic Roasted Parsnip 139

Traditional Baba Ganoush 142

Peanut Butter Date Bites 144

Roasted Cauliflower Dip 145

Easy Zucchini Roll-Ups 147

Chipotle Sweet Potato Fries 149

Cannellini Bean Dipping Sauce 151

Spiced Roasted Cauliflower 153

Easy Lebanese Toum 156

Avocado with Tangy Ginger Dressing 158

Chickpea Snack Mix 160

Muhammara Dip with a Twist 162

Spinach, Chickpea and Garlic Crostini 164

Mushroom and Cannellini Bean "Meatballs" 167

Cucumber Rounds with Hummus 169

Stuffed Jalapeño Bites 170

Mexican-Style Onion Rings 172

Roasted Root Vegetables 174

Indian-Style Hummus Dip 176

Roasted Carrot and Bean Dip 178

Quick and Easy Zucchini Sushi 180

Cherry Tomatoes with Hummus 182

Oven-Roasted Button Mushrooms 184

Cheesy Kale Chips 187

Hummus Avocado Boats 189

Nacho Stuffed Button Mushrooms 191

Lettuce Wraps with Hummus and Avocado 193

Roasted Brussels Sprouts 195

Sweet Potato Poblano Poppers 197

Baked Zucchini Chips 199

Authentic Lebanese Dip 201

Oat Vegan Meatballs 203

Bell Pepper Boats with Mango Salsa 205

Tangy Rosemary Broccoli Florets 207

Crispy Baked Beetroot Chips 209

Red Kidney Bean Salad 210

Anasazi Bean and Vegetable Stew 212

Easy and Hearty Shakshuka 214

Old-Fashioned Chili 216

Easy Red Lentil Salad 218

Introduciton

It is only until recently that more and more people are starting to embrace the plant-based diet lifestyle. As to what exactly has drawn tens of millions of people into this lifestyle is debatable. However, there is growing evidence demonstrating that following a primarily plant-based diet lifestyle leads to better weight control and general health, free of many chronic diseases. What are the Health Benefits of a Plant-Based Diet? As it turns out, eating plant-based is one of the healthiest diets in the world. Healthy vegan diets include plenty of fresh products, whole grains, legumes, and healthy fats such as seeds and nuts. They are abundant with antioxidants, minerals, vitamins, and dietary fiber. Current scientific researches pointed out that higher consumption of plant-based foods is associated with a lower risk of mortality from conditions such as cardiovascular disease, type 2 diabetes, hypertension, and obesity. Vegan eating plans often rely heavily on healthy staples, avoiding animal products that are loaded with antibiotics, additives, and hormones. Plus, consuming a higher proportion of essential amino acids with animal protein can be damaging to human health. Since animal products contain much 8 more fat than plant-based foods, it's not a shocker that studies have shown that meat-eaters have nine times the obesity rate of vegans. This leads us to the next point, one of the greatest benefits of the vegan diet – weight loss. While many people choose to live a vegan life for ethical reasons, the diet itself can help you achieve your weight loss goals. If you're struggling to shift pounds, you may want to consider trying a plant-based diet. How exactly? As a vegan, you will reduce the number of high-calorie foods such as full-fat dairy products, fatty fish, pork and other cholesterol containing foods such as eggs. Try replacing such foods with high fiber and protein-rich alternatives that will keep you fuller longer. The key is focusing on nutrient-dense, clean and natural foods and avoid empty calories such as sugar, saturated fats, and highly processed foods. Here are a few tricks that help me maintain my weight on the vegan diet for years. I eat vegetables as a main course; I consume good fats in moderation – a good fat such as olive oil does not make you fat; I exercise regularly and cook at home. Enjoy!

RICE & GRAINS

Classic Garlicky Rice

(Ready in about 20 minutes | Servings 4)

Per serving : Calories: 422; Fat: 15.1g; Carbs: 61.1g; Protein: 9.3g

Ingredients

  4 tablespoons olive oil

  4 cloves garlic, chopped

  1 ½ cups white rice

  2 ½ cups vegetable broth

Directions

In a saucepan, heat the olive oil over a moderately high flame. Add in the garlic and sauté for about 1 minute or until aromatic.

Add in the rice and broth. Bring to a boil; immediately turn the heat to a gentle simmer.

Cook for about 15 minutes or until all the liquid has absorbed. Fluff the rice with a fork, season with salt and pepper and serve hot!

Brown Rice with Vegetables and Tofu

(Ready in about 45 minutes | Servings 4)

Per serving : Calories: 410; Fat: 13.2g; Carbs: 60g; Protein: 14.3g

Ingredients

 4 teaspoons sesame seeds

 2 spring garlic stalks, minced

 1 cup spring onions, chopped

 1 carrot, trimmed and sliced

 1 celery rib, sliced

 1/4 cup dry white wine

 10 ounces tofu, cubed

 1 ½ cups long-grain brown rice, rinsed thoroughly

 2 tablespoons soy sauce

 2 tablespoons tahini

 1 tablespoon lemon juice

Directions

In a wok or large saucepan, heat 2 teaspoons of the sesame oil over medium-high heat. Now, cook the garlic, onion, carrot and celery for about 3 minutes, stirring periodically to ensure even cooking.

Add the wine to deglaze the pan and push the vegetables to one side of the wok. Add in the remaining sesame oil and fry the tofu for 8 minutes, stirring occasionally.

Bring 2 ½ cups of water to a boil over medium-high heat. Bring to a simmer and cook the rice for about 30 minutes or until it is tender; fluff the rice and stir it with the soy sauce and tahini.

Stir the vegetables and tofu into the hot rice; add a few drizzles of the fresh lemon juice and serve warm. Bon appétit!

Basic Amaranth Porridge

(Ready in about 35 minutes | Servings 4)

Per serving : Calories: 261; Fat: 4.4g; Carbs: 49g; Protein: 7.3g

Ingredients

3 cups water

1 cup amaranth

1/2 cup coconut milk

4 tablespoons agave syrup

A pinch of kosher salt

A pinch of grated nutmeg

Directions

Bring the water to a boil over medium-high heat; add in the amaranth and turn the heat to a simmer.

Let it cook for about 30 minutes, stirring periodically to prevent the amaranth from sticking to the bottom of the pan.

Stir in the remaining ingredients and continue to cook for 1 to 2 minutes more until cooked through. Bon appétit!

. Country Cornbread with Spinach

(Ready in about 50 minutes | Servings 8)

Per serving : Calories: 282; Fat: 15.4g; Carbs: 30g; Protein: 4.6g

Ingredients

1 tablespoon flaxseed meal

1 cup all-purpose flour

1 cup yellow cornmeal

1/2 teaspoon baking soda

1/2 teaspoon baking powder

1 teaspoon kosher salt

1 teaspoon brown sugar

A pinch of grated nutmeg

1 ¼ cups oat milk, unsweetened

1 teaspoon white vinegar

1/2 cup olive oil

2 cups spinach, torn into pieces

Directions

Start by preheating your oven to 420 degrees F. Now, spritz a baking pan with a nonstick cooking spray.

To make the flax eggs, mix flaxseed meal with 3 tablespoons of the water. Stir and let it sit for about 15 minutes.

In a mixing bowl, thoroughly combine the flour, cornmeal, baking soda, baking powder, salt, sugar and grated nutmeg.

Gradually add in the flax egg, oat milk, vinegar and olive oil, whisking constantly to avoid lumps. Afterwards, fold in the spinach.

Scrape the batter into the prepared baking pan. Bake your cornbread for about 25 minutes or until a tester inserted in the middle comes out dry and clean.

Let it stand for about 10 minutes before slicing and serving. Bon appétit!

Rice Pudding with Currants

(Ready in about 45 minutes | Servings 4)

Per serving : Calories: 423; Fat: 5.3g; Carbs: 85g; Protein: 8.8g

Ingredients

1 ½ cups water

1 cup white rice

2 ½ cups oat milk, divided

1/2 cup white sugar

A pinch of salt

A pinch of grated nutmeg

1 teaspoon ground cinnamon

1/2 teaspoon vanilla extract

1/2 cup dried currants

Directions

In a saucepan, bring the water to a boil over medium-high heat. Immediately turn the heat to a simmer, add in the rice and let it cook for about 20 minutes.

Add in the milk, sugar and spices and continue to cook for 20 minutes more, stirring constantly to prevent the rice from sticking to the pan.

Top with dried currants and serve at room temperature. Bon appétit!

Millet Porridge with Sultanas

(Ready in about 25 minutes | Servings 3)

Per serving : Calories: 353; Fat: 5.5g; Carbs: 65.2g; Protein: 9.8g

Ingredients

1 cup water

1 cup coconut milk

1 cup millet, rinsed

1/4 teaspoon grated nutmeg

1/4 teaspoon ground cinnamon

1 teaspoon vanilla paste

1/4 teaspoon kosher salt

2 tablespoons agave syrup

4 tablespoons sultana raisins

Directions

Place the water, milk, millet, nutmeg, cinnamon, vanilla and salt in a saucepan; bring to a boil.

Turn the heat to a simmer and let it cook for about 20 minutes; fluff the millet with a fork and spoon into individual bowls.

Serve with agave syrup and sultanas. Bon appétit!

Quinoa Porridge with Dried Figs

(Ready in about 25 minutes | Servings 3)

Per serving : Calories: 414; Fat: 9g; Carbs: 71.2g; Protein: 13.8g

Ingredients

1 cup white quinoa, rinsed

2 cups almond milk

4 tablespoons brown sugar

A pinch of salt

1/4 teaspoon grated nutmeg

1/2 teaspoon ground cinnamon

1/2 teaspoon vanilla extract

1/2 cup dried figs, chopped

Directions

Place the quinoa, almond milk, sugar, salt, nutmeg, cinnamon and vanilla extract in a saucepan.

Bring it to a boil over medium-high heat. Turn the heat to a simmer and let it cook for about 20 minutes; fluff with a fork.

Divide between three serving bowls and garnish with dried figs. Bon appétit!

Bread Pudding with Raisins

(Ready in about 1 hour | Servings 4)

Per serving : Calories: 474; Fat: 12.2g; Carbs: 72g; Protein: 14.4g

Ingredients

4 cups day-old bread, cubed

1 cup brown sugar

4 cups coconut milk

1/2 teaspoon vanilla extract

1 teaspoon ground cinnamon

2 tablespoons rum

1/2 cup raisins

Directions

Start by preheating your oven to 360 degrees F. Lightly oil a casserole dish with a nonstick cooking spray.

Place the cubed bread in the prepared casserole dish.

In a mixing bowl, thoroughly combine the sugar, milk, vanilla, cinnamon, rum and raisins. Pour the custard evenly over the bread cubes.

Let it soak for about 15 minutes.

Bake in the preheated oven for about 45 minutes or until the top is golden and set. Bon appétit!

Bulgur Wheat Salad

(Ready in about 25 minutes | Servings 4)

Per serving : Calories: 359; Fat: 15.5g; Carbs: 48.1g; Protein: 10.1g

Ingredients

1 cup bulgur wheat

1 ½ cups vegetable broth

1 teaspoon sea salt

1 teaspoon fresh ginger, minced

4 tablespoons olive oil

1 onion, chopped

8 ounces canned garbanzo beans, drained

2 large roasted peppers, sliced

2 tablespoons fresh parsley, roughly chopped

Directions

In a deep saucepan, bring the bulgur wheat and vegetable broth to a simmer; let it cook, covered, for 12 to 13 minutes.

Let it stand for about 10 minutes and fluff with a fork.

Add the remaining ingredients to the cooked bulgur wheat; serve at room temperature or well-chilled. Bon appétit!

Rye Porridge with Blueberry Topping

(Ready in about 15 minutes | Servings 3)

Per serving : Calories: 359; Fat: 11g; Carbs: 56.1g; Protein: 12.1g

Ingredients

 1 cup rye flakes

 1 cup water

 1 cup coconut milk

 1 cup fresh blueberries

 1 tablespoon coconut oil

 6 dates, pitted

Directions

Add the rye flakes, water and coconut milk to a deep saucepan; bring to a boil over medium-high. Turn the heat to a simmer and let it cook for 5 to 6 minutes.

In a blender or food processor, puree the blueberries with the coconut oil and dates.

Ladle into three bowls and garnish with the blueberry topping.

Bon appétit!

Coconut Sorghum Porridge

(Ready in about 15 minutes | Servings 2)

Per serving : Calories: 289; Fat: 5.1g; Carbs: 57.8g; Protein: 7.3g

Ingredients

1/2 cup sorghum

1 cup water

1/2 cup coconut milk

1/4 teaspoon grated nutmeg

1/4 teaspoon ground cloves

1/2 teaspoon ground cinnamon

Kosher salt, to taste

2 tablespoons agave syrup

2 tablespoons coconut flakes

Directions

Place the sorghum, water, milk, nutmeg, cloves, cinnamon and kosher salt in a saucepan; simmer gently for about 15 minutes.

Spoon the porridge into serving bowls. Top with agave syrup and coconut flakes. Bon appétit!

Dad's Aromatic Rice

(Ready in about 20 minutes | Servings 4)

Per serving : Calories: 384; Fat: 11.4g; Carbs: 60.4g; Protein: 8.3g

Ingredients

3 tablespoons olive oil

1 teaspoon garlic, minced

1 teaspoon dried oregano

1 teaspoon dried rosemary

1 bay leaf

1 ½ cups white rice

2 ½ cups vegetable broth

Sea salt and cayenne pepper, to taste

Directions

In a saucepan, heat the olive oil over a moderately high flame. Add in the garlic, oregano, rosemary and bay leaf; sauté for about 1 minute or until aromatic.

Add in the rice and broth. Bring to a boil; immediately turn the heat to a gentle simmer.

Cook for about 15 minutes or until all the liquid has absorbed. Fluff the rice with a fork, season with salt and pepper and serve immediately.

Bon appétit!

Everyday Savory Grits

(Ready in about 35 minutes | Servings 4)

Per serving : Calories: 238; Fat: 6.5g; Carbs: 38.7g; Protein: 3.7g

Ingredients

2 tablespoons vegan butter

1 sweet onion, chopped

1 teaspoon garlic, minced

4 cups water

1 cup stone-ground grits

Sea salt and cayenne pepper, to taste

Directions

In a saucepan, melt the vegan butter over medium-high heat. Once hot, cook the onion for about 3 minutes or until tender.

Add in the garlic and continue to sauté for 30 seconds more or until aromatic; reserve.

Bring the water to a boil over a moderately high heat. Stir in the grits, salt and pepper. Turn the heat to a simmer, cover and continue to cook, for about 30 minutes or until cooked through.

Stir in the sautéed mixture and serve warm. Bon appétit!

Greek-Style Barley Salad

(Ready in about 35 minutes | Servings 4)

Per serving : Calories: 378; Fat: 15.6g; Carbs: 50g; Protein: 10.7g

Ingredients

1 cup pearl barley

2 ¾ cups vegetable broth

2 tablespoons apple cider vinegar

4 tablespoons extra-virgin olive oil

2 bell peppers, seeded and diced

1 shallot, chopped

2 ounces sun-dried tomatoes in oil, chopped

1/2 green olives, pitted and sliced

2 tablespoons fresh cilantro, roughly chopped

Directions

Bring the barley and broth to a boil over medium-high heat; now, turn the heat to a simmer.

Continue to simmer for about 30 minutes until all the liquid has absorbed; fluff with a fork.

Toss the barley with the vinegar, olive oil, peppers, shallots, sun-dried tomatoes and olives; toss to combine well.

Garnish with fresh cilantro and serve at room temperature or well-chilled. Enjoy!

Easy Sweet Maize Meal Porridge

(Ready in about 15 minutes | Servings 2)

Per serving : Calories: 278; Fat: 12.7g; Carbs: 37.2g; Protein: 3g

Ingredients

- 2 cups water
- 1/2 cup maize meal
- 1/4 teaspoon ground allspice
- 1/4 teaspoon salt
- 2 tablespoons brown sugar
- 2 tablespoons almond butter

Directions

In a saucepan, bring the water to a boil; then, gradually add in the maize meal and turn the heat to a simmer.

Add in the ground allspice and salt. Let it cook for 10 minutes.

Add in the brown sugar and almond butter and gently stir to combine. Bon appétit!

Mom's Millet Muffins

(Ready in about 20 minutes | Servings 8)

Per serving : Calories: 367; Fat: 15.9g; Carbs: 53.7g; Protein: 6.5g

Ingredients

2 cup whole-wheat flour

1/2 cup millet

2 teaspoons baking powder

1/2 teaspoon salt

1 cup coconut milk

1/2 cup coconut oil, melted

1/2 cup agave nectar

1/2 teaspoon ground cinnamon

1/4 teaspoon ground cloves

A pinch of grated nutmeg

1/2 cup dried apricots, chopped

Directions

Begin by preheating your oven to 400 degrees F. Lightly oil a muffin tin with a nonstick oil.

In a mixing bowl, mix all dry ingredients. In a separate bowl, mix the wet ingredients. Stir the milk mixture into the flour mixture; mix just until evenly moist and do not overmix your batter.

Fold in the apricots and scrape the batter into the prepared muffin cups.

Bake the muffins in the preheated oven for about 15 minutes, or until a tester inserted in the center of your muffin comes out dry and clean.

Let it stand for 10 minutes on a wire rack before unmolding and serving. Enjoy!

Ginger Brown Rice

(Ready in about 30 minutes | Servings 4)

Per serving : Calories: 318; Fat: 8.8g; Carbs: 53.4g; Protein: 5.6g

Ingredients

1 ½ cups brown rice, rinsed

2 tablespoons olive oil

1 teaspoon garlic, minced

1 (1-inch) piece ginger, peeled and minced

1/2 teaspoon cumin seeds

Sea salt and ground black pepper, to taste

Directions

Place the brown rice in a saucepan and cover with cold water by 2 inches. Bring to a boil.

Turn the heat to a simmer and continue to cook for about 30 minutes or until tender.

In a sauté pan, heat the olive oil over medium-high heat. Once hot, cook the garlic, ginger and cumin seeds until aromatic.

Stir the garlic/ginger mixture into the hot rice; season with salt and pepper and serve immediately. Bon appétit!

Sweet Oatmeal "Grits"

(Ready in about 20 minutes | Servings 4)

Per serving : Calories: 380; Fat: 11.1g; Carbs: 59g; Protein: 14.4g

Ingredients

1 ½ cups steel-cut oats, soaked overnight

1 cup almond milk

2 cups water

A pinch of grated nutmeg

A pinch of ground cloves

A pinch of sea salt

4 tablespoons almonds, slivered

6 dates, pitted and chopped

6 prunes, chopped

Directions

In a deep saucepan, bring the steel cut oats, almond milk and water to a boil.

Add in the nutmeg, cloves and salt. Immediately turn the heat to a simmer, cover and continue to cook for about 15 minutes or until they've softened.

Then, spoon the grits into four serving bowls; top them with the almonds, dates and prunes.

Bon appétit!

Freekeh Bowl with Dried Figs

(Ready in about 35 minutes | Servings 2)

Per serving : Calories: 458; Fat: 6.8g; Carbs: 90g; Protein: 12.4g

Ingredients

1/2 cup freekeh, soaked for 30 minutes, drained

1 1/3 cups almond milk

1/4 teaspoon sea salt

1/4 teaspoon ground cloves

1/4 teaspoon ground cinnamon

4 tablespoons agave syrup

2 ounces dried figs, chopped

Directions

Place the freekeh, milk, sea salt, ground cloves and cinnamon in a saucepan. Bring to a boil over medium-high heat.

Immediately turn the heat to a simmer for 30 to 35 minutes, stirring occasionally to promote even cooking.

Stir in the agave syrup and figs. Ladle the porridge into individual bowls and serve. Bon appétit!

Cornmeal Porridge with Maple Syrup

(Ready in about 20 minutes | Servings 4)

Per serving : Calories: 328; Fat: 4.8g; Carbs: 63.4g; Protein: 6.6g

Ingredients

2 cups water

2 cups almond milk

1 cinnamon stick

1 vanilla bean

1 cup yellow cornmeal

1/2 cup maple syrup

Directions

In a saucepan, bring the water and almond milk to a boil. Add in the cinnamon stick and vanilla bean.

Gradually add in the cornmeal, stirring continuously; turn the heat to a simmer. Let it simmer for about 15 minutes.

Drizzle the maple syrup over the porridge and serve warm. Enjoy!

Mediterranean-Style Rice

(Ready in about 20 minutes | Servings 4)

Per serving : Calories: 403; Fat: 12g; Carbs: 64.1g; Protein: 8.3g

Ingredients

3 tablespoons vegan butter, at room temperature

4 tablespoons scallions, chopped

2 cloves garlic, minced

1 bay leaf

1 thyme sprig, chopped

1 rosemary sprig, chopped

1 ½ cups white rice

2 cups vegetable broth

1 large tomato, pureed

Sea salt and ground black pepper, to taste

2 ounces Kalamata olives, pitted and sliced

Directions

In a saucepan, melt the vegan butter over a moderately high flame. Cook the scallions for about 2 minutes or until tender.

Add in the garlic, bay leaf, thyme and rosemary and continue to sauté for about 1 minute or until aromatic.

Add in the rice, broth and pureed tomato. Bring to a boil; immediately turn the heat to a gentle simmer.

Cook for about 15 minutes or until all the liquid has absorbed. Fluff the rice with a fork, season with salt and pepper and garnish with olives; serve immediately.

Bon appétit!

Bulgur Pancakes with a Twist

(Ready in about 50 minutes | Servings 4)

Per serving : Calories: 414; Fat: 21.8g; Carbs: 51.8g; Protein: 6.5g

Ingredients

1/2 cup bulgur wheat flour

1/2 cup almond flour

1 teaspoon baking soda

1/2 teaspoon fine sea salt

1 cup full-fat coconut milk

1/2 teaspoon ground cinnamon

1/4 teaspoon ground cloves

4 tablespoons coconut oil

1/2 cup maple syrup

1 large-sized banana, sliced

Directions

In a mixing bowl, thoroughly combine the flour, baking soda, salt, coconut milk, cinnamon and ground cloves; let it stand for 30 minutes to soak well.

Heat a small amount of the coconut oil in a frying pan.

Fry the pancakes until the surface is golden brown. Garnish with maple syrup and banana. Bon appétit!

Chocolate Rye Porridge

(Ready in about 10 minutes | Servings 4)

Per serving : Calories: 460; Fat: 13.1g; Carbs: 72.2g; Protein: 15g

Ingredients

2 cups rye flakes

2 ½ cups almond milk

2 ounces dried prunes, chopped

2 ounces dark chocolate chunks

Directions

Add the rye flakes and almond milk to a deep saucepan; bring to a boil over medium-high. Turn the heat to a simmer and let it cook for 5 to 6 minutes.

Remove from the heat. Fold in the chopped prunes and chocolate chunks, gently stir to combine.

Ladle into serving bowls and serve warm.

Bon appétit!

Authentic African Mielie-Meal

(Ready in about 15 minutes | Servings 4)

Per serving : Calories: 336; Fat: 15.1g; Carbs: 47.9g; Protein: 4.1g

Ingredients

3 cups water

1 cup coconut milk

1 cup maize meal

1/3 teaspoon kosher salt

1/4 teaspoon grated nutmeg

1/4 teaspoon ground cloves

4 tablespoons maple syrup

Directions

In a saucepan, bring the water and milk to a boil; then, gradually add in the maize meal and turn the heat to a simmer.

Add in the salt, nutmeg and cloves. Let it cook for 10 minutes.

Add in the maple syrup and gently stir to combine. Bon appétit!

Teff Porridge with Dried Figs

(Ready in about 25 minutes | Servings 4)

Per serving : Calories: 356; Fat: 12.1g; Carbs: 56.5g; Protein: 6.8g

Ingredients

1 cup whole-grain teff

1 cup water

2 cups coconut milk

2 tablespoons coconut oil

1/2 teaspoon ground cardamom

1/4 teaspoon ground cinnamon

4 tablespoons agave syrup

7-8 dried figs, chopped

Directions

Bring the whole-grain teff, water and coconut milk to a boil.

Turn the heat to a simmer and add in the coconut oil, cardamom and cinnamon.

Let it cook for 20 minutes or until the grain has softened and the porridge has thickened. Stir in the agave syrup and stir to combine well.

Top each serving bowl with chopped figs and serve warm. Bon appétit!

Decadent Bread Pudding with Apricots

(Ready in about 1 hour | Servings 4)

Per serving : Calories: 418; Fat: 18.8g; Carbs: 56.9g; Protein: 7.3g

Ingredients

4 cups day-old ciabatta bread, cubed

4 tablespoons coconut oil, melted

2 cups coconut milk

1/2 cup coconut sugar

4 tablespoons applesauce

1/4 teaspoon ground cloves

1/2 teaspoon ground cinnamon

1 teaspoon vanilla extract

1/3 cup dried apricots, diced

Directions

Start by preheating your oven to 360 degrees F. Lightly oil a casserole dish with a nonstick cooking spray.

Place the cubed bread in the prepared casserole dish.

In a mixing bowl, thoroughly combine the coconut oil, milk, coconut sugar, applesauce, ground cloves, ground cinnamon and vanilla. Pour the custard evenly over the bread cubes; fold in the apricots.

Press with a wide spatula and let it soak for about 15 minutes.

Bake in the preheated oven for about 45 minutes or until the top is golden and set. Bon appétit!

Chipotle Cilantro Rice

(Ready in about 25 minutes | Servings 4)

Per serving : Calories: 313; Fat: 15g; Carbs: 37.1g; Protein: 5.7g

Ingredients

4 tablespoons olive oil

1 chipotle pepper, seeded and chopped

1 cup jasmine rice

1 ½ cups vegetable broth

1/4 cup fresh cilantro, chopped

Sea salt and cayenne pepper, to taste

Directions

In a saucepan, heat the olive oil over a moderately high flame. Add in the pepper and rice and cook for about 3 minutes or until aromatic.

Pour the vegetable broth into the saucepan and bring to a boil; immediately turn the heat to a gentle simmer.

Cook for about 18 minutes or until all the liquid has absorbed. Fluff the rice with a fork, add in the cilantro, salt and cayenne pepper; stir to combine well. Bon appétit!

Oat Porridge with Almonds

(Ready in about 20 minutes | Servings 2)

Per serving : Calories: 533; Fat: 13.7g; Carbs: 85g; Protein: 21.6g

Ingredients

1 cup water

2 cups almond milk, divided

1 cup rolled oats

2 tablespoons coconut sugar

1/2 vanilla essence

1/4 teaspoon cardamom

1/2 cup almonds, chopped

1 banana, sliced

Directions

In a deep saucepan, bring the water and milk to a rapid boil. Add in the oats, cover the saucepan and turn the heat to medium.

Add in the coconut sugar, vanilla and cardamom. Continue to cook for about 12 minutes, stirring periodically.

Spoon the mixture into serving bowls; top with almonds and banana. Bon appétit!

Aromatic Millet Bowl

(Ready in about 20 minutes | Servings 3)

Per serving : Calories: 363; Fat: 6.7g; Carbs: 63.5g; Protein: 11.6g

Ingredients

1 cup water

1 ½ cups coconut milk

1 cup millet, rinsed and drained

1/4 teaspoon crystallized ginger

1/4 teaspoon ground cinnamon

A pinch of grated nutmeg

A pinch of Himalayan salt

2 tablespoons maple syrup

Directions

Place the water, milk, millet, crystallized ginger cinnamon, nutmeg and salt in a saucepan; bring to a boil.

Turn the heat to a simmer and let it cook for about 20 minutes; fluff the millet with a fork and spoon into individual bowls.

Serve with maple syrup. Bon appétit!

Harissa Bulgur Bowl

(Ready in about 25 minutes | Servings 4)

Per serving : Calories: 353; Fat: 15.5g; Carbs: 48.5g; Protein: 8.4g

Ingredients

1 cup bulgur wheat

1 ½ cups vegetable broth

2 cups sweet corn kernels, thawed

1 cup canned kidney beans, drained

1 red onion, thinly sliced

1 garlic clove, minced

Sea salt and ground black pepper, to taste

1/4 cup harissa paste

1 tablespoon lemon juice

1 tablespoon white vinegar

1/4 cup extra-virgin olive oil

1/4 cup fresh parsley leaves, roughly chopped

Directions

In a deep saucepan, bring the bulgur wheat and vegetable broth to a simmer; let it cook, covered, for 12 to 13 minutes.

Let it stand for 5 to 10 minutes and fluff your bulgur with a fork.

Add the remaining ingredients to the cooked bulgur wheat; serve warm or at room temperature. Bon appétit!

Coconut Quinoa Pudding

(Ready in about 20 minutes | Servings 3)

Per serving : Calories: 391; Fat: 10.6g; Carbs: 65.2g; Protein: 11.1g

Ingredients

1 cup water

1 cup coconut milk

1 cup quinoa

A pinch of kosher salt

A pinch of ground allspice

1/2 teaspoon cinnamon

1/2 teaspoon vanilla extract

4 tablespoons agave syrup

1/2 cup coconut flakes

Directions

Place the water, coconut milk, quinoa, salt, ground allspice, cinnamon and vanilla extract in a saucepan.

Bring it to a boil over medium-high heat. Turn the heat to a simmer and let it cook for about 20 minutes; fluff with a fork and add in the agave syrup.

Divide between three serving bowls and garnish with coconut flakes. Bon appétit!

Cremini Mushroom Risotto

(Ready in about 20 minutes | Servings 3)

Per serving : Calories: 513; Fat: 12.5g; Carbs: 88g; Protein: 11.7g

Ingredients

3 tablespoons vegan butter

1 teaspoon garlic, minced

1 teaspoon thyme

1 pound Cremini mushrooms, sliced

1 ½ cups white rice

2 ½ cups vegetable broth

1/4 cup dry sherry wine

Kosher salt and ground black pepper, to taste

3 tablespoons fresh scallions, thinly sliced

Directions

In a saucepan, melt the vegan butter over a moderately high flame. Cook the garlic and thyme for about 1 minute or until aromatic.

Add in the mushrooms and continue to sauté until they release the liquid or about 3 minutes.

Add in the rice, vegetable broth and sherry wine. Bring to a boil; immediately turn the heat to a gentle simmer.

Cook for about 15 minutes or until all the liquid has absorbed. Fluff the rice with a fork, season with salt and pepper and garnish with fresh scallions.

Bon appétit!

Colorful Risotto with Vegetables

(Ready in about 35 minutes | Servings 5)

Per serving : Calories: 363; Fat: 7.5g; Carbs: 66.3g; Protein: 7.7g

Ingredients

2 tablespoons sesame oil

1 onion, chopped

2 bell peppers, chopped

1 parsnip, trimmed and chopped

1 carrot, trimmed and chopped

1 cup broccoli florets

2 garlic cloves, finely chopped

1/2 teaspoon ground cumin

2 cups brown rice

Sea salt and black pepper, to taste

1/2 teaspoon ground turmeric

2 tablespoons fresh cilantro, finely chopped

Directions

Heat the sesame oil in a saucepan over medium-high heat.

Once hot, cook the onion, peppers, parsnip, carrot and broccoli for about 3 minutes until aromatic.

Add in the garlic and ground cumin; continue to cook for 30 seconds more until aromatic.

Place the brown rice in a saucepan and cover with cold water by 2 inches. Bring to a boil. Turn the heat to a simmer and continue to cook for about 30 minutes or until tender.

Stir the rice into the vegetable mixture; season with salt, black pepper and ground turmeric; garnish with fresh cilantro and serve immediately. Bon appétit!

Amarant Grits with Walnuts

(Ready in about 35 minutes | Servings 4)

Per serving : Calories: 356; Fat: 12g; Carbs: 51.3g; Protein: 12.2g

Ingredients

2 cups water

2 cups coconut milk

1 cup amaranth

1 cinnamon stick

1 vanilla bean

4 tablespoons maple syrup

4 tablespoons walnuts, chopped

Directions

Bring the water and coconut milk to a boil over medium-high heat; add in the amaranth, cinnamon and vanilla and turn the heat to a simmer.

Let it cook for about 30 minutes, stirring periodically to prevent the amaranth from sticking to the bottom of the pan.

Top with maple syrup and walnuts. Bon appétit!

Barley Pilaf with Wild Mushrooms

(Ready in about 45 minutes | Servings 4)

Per serving : Calories: 288; Fat: 7.7g; Carbs: 45.3g; Protein: 12.1g

Ingredients

2 tablespoons vegan butter

1 small onion, chopped

1 teaspoon garlic, minced

1 jalapeno pepper, seeded and minced

1 pound wild mushrooms, sliced

1 cup medium pearl barley, rinsed

2 ¾ cups vegetable broth

Directions

Melt the vegan butter in a saucepan over medium-high heat.

Once hot, cook the onion for about 3 minutes until just tender.

Add in the garlic, jalapeno pepper, mushrooms; continue to sauté for 2 minutes or until aromatic.

Add in the barley and broth, cover and continue to simmer for about 30 minutes. Once all the liquid has absorbed, allow the barley to rest for about 10 minutes fluff with a fork.

Taste and adjust the seasonings. Bon appétit!

Sweet Cornbread Muffins

(Ready in about 30 minutes | Servings 8)

Per serving : Calories: 311; Fat: 13.7g; Carbs: 42.3g; Protein: 4.5g

Ingredients

1 cup all-purpose flour

1 cup yellow cornmeal

1 teaspoon baking powder

1 teaspoon baking soda

1 teaspoon kosher salt

1/2 cup sugar

1/2 teaspoon ground cinnamon

1 1/2 cups almond milk

1/2 cup vegan butter, melted

2 tablespoons applesauce

Directions

Start by preheating your oven to 420 degrees F. Now, spritz a muffin tin with a nonstick cooking spray.

In a mixing bowl, thoroughly combine the flour, cornmeal, baking soda, baking powder, salt, sugar and cinnamon.

Gradually add in the milk, butter and applesauce, whisking constantly to avoid lumps.

Scrape the batter into the prepared muffin tin. Bake your muffins for about 25 minutes or until a tester inserted in the middle comes out dry and clean.

Transfer them to a wire rack to rest for 5 minutes before unmolding and serving. Bon appétit!

Aromatic Rice Pudding with Dried Figs

(Ready in about 45 minutes | Servings 4)

Per serving : Calories: 407; Fat: 7.5g; Carbs: 74.3g; Protein: 10.7g

Ingredients

2 cups water

1 cup medium-grain white rice

3 ½ cups coconut milk

1/2 cup coconut sugar

1 cinnamon stick

1 vanilla bean

1/2 cup dried figs, chopped

4 tablespoons coconut, shredded

Directions

In a saucepan, bring the water to a boil over medium-high heat. Immediately turn the heat to a simmer, add in the rice and let it cook for about 20 minutes.

Add in the milk, sugar and spices and continue to cook for 20 minutes more, stirring constantly to prevent the rice from sticking to the pan.

Top with dried figs and coconut; serve your pudding warm or at room temperature. Bon appétit!

Potage au Quinoa

(Ready in about 25 minutes | Servings 4)

Per serving : Calories: 466; Fat: 11.1g; Carbs: 76g; Protein: 16.1g

Ingredients

2 tablespoons olive oil

1 onion, chopped

4 medium potatoes, peeled and diced

1 carrot, trimmed and diced

1 parsnip, trimmed and diced

1 jalapeno pepper, seeded and chopped

4 cups vegetable broth

1 cup quinoa

Sea salt and ground white pepper, to taste

Directions

In a heavy-bottomed pot, heat the olive oil over medium-high heat. Sauté the onion, potatoes, carrots, parsnip and pepper for about 5 minutes or until they've softened.

Add in the vegetable broth and quinoa; bring to a boil.

Immediately turn the heat to a simmer for about 15 minutes or until the quinoa is tender.

Season with salt and pepper to taste. Puree your potage with an immersion blender. Reheat the potage just before serving and enjoy!

Sorghum Bowl with Almonds

(Ready in about 15 minutes | Servings 4)

Per serving : Calories: 384; Fat: 14.7g; Carbs: 54.6g; Protein: 13.9g

Ingredients

1 cup sorghum

3 cups almond milk

A pinch of sea salt

A pinch of grated nutmeg

1/2 teaspoon ground cinnamon

1/4 teaspoon ground cardamom

1 teaspoon crystallized ginger

4 tablespoons brown sugar

4 tablespoons almonds, slivered

Directions

Place the sorghum, almond milk, salt, nutmeg, cinnamon, cardamom and crystallized ginger in a saucepan; simmer gently for about 15 minutes.

Add in the brown sugar, stir and spoon the porridge into serving bowls.

Top with almonds and serve immediately. Bon appétit!

Bulgur Muffins with Raisins

(Ready in about 20 minutes | Servings 6)

Per serving : Calories: 306; Fat: 12.1g; Carbs: 44.6g; Protein: 6.1g

Ingredients

1 cup bulgur, cooked

4 tablespoons coconut oil, melted

1 teaspoon baking powder

1 teaspoon baking soda

2 tablespoons flax egg

1 ¼ cups all-purpose flour

1/2 cup coconut flour

1 cup coconut milk

4 tablespoons brown sugar

1/2 cup raisins, packed

Directions

Start by preheating your oven to 420 degrees F. Spritz a muffin tin with a nonstick cooking oil.

Thoroughly combine all the dry ingredients. Add in the cooked bulgur.

In another bowl, whisk all the wet ingredients; add the wet mixture to the bulgur mixture; fold in the raisins.

Mix until everything is well combined, but not overmixed; spoon the batter into the prepared muffin.

Now, bake your muffins for about 16 minutes or until a tester comes out dry and clean. Bon appétit!

Old-Fashioned Pilaf

(Ready in about 45 minutes | Servings 4)

Per serving : Calories: 532; Fat: 11.4g; Carbs: 93g; Protein: 16.3g

Ingredients

2 tablespoons sesame oil

1 shallot, sliced

2 bell peppers, seeded and sliced

3 cloves garlic, minced

10 ounces oyster mushrooms, cleaned and sliced

2 cups brown rice

2 tomatoes, pureed

2 cups vegetable broth

Salt and black pepper, to taste

1 cup sweet corn kernels

1 cup green peas

Directions

Heat the sesame oil in a saucepan over medium-high heat.

Once hot, cook the shallot and peppers for about 3 minutes until just tender.

Add in the garlic and oyster mushrooms; continue to sauté for 1 minute or so until aromatic.

In a lightly oiled casserole dish, place the rice, flowed by the mushroom mixture, tomatoes, broth, salt, black pepper, corn and green peas.

Bake, covered, at 375 degrees F for about 40 minutes, stirring after 20 minutes. Bon appétit!

Freekeh Salad with Za'atar

(Ready in about 35 minutes | Servings 4)

Per serving : Calories: 352; Fat: 17.1g; Carbs: 46.3g; Protein: 8g

Ingredients

1 cup freekeh

2 ½ cups water

1 cup grape tomatoes, halved

2 bell peppers, seeded and sliced

1 habanero pepper, seeded and sliced

1 onion, thinly sliced

2 tablespoons fresh cilantro, chopped

2 tablespoons fresh parsley, chopped

2 ounces green olives, pitted and sliced

1/4 cup extra-virgin olive oil

2 tablespoons lemon juice

1 teaspoon deli mustard

1 teaspoon za'atar

Sea salt and ground black pepper, to taste

Directions

Place the freekeh and water in a saucepan. Bring to a boil over medium-high heat.

Immediately turn the heat to a simmer for 30 to 35 minutes, stirring occasionally to promote even cooking. Let it cool completely.

Toss the cooked freekeh with the remaining ingredients. Toss to combine well.

Bon appétit!

Vegetable Amaranth Soup

(Ready in about 30 minutes | Servings 4)

Per serving : Calories: 196; Fat: 8.7g; Carbs: 26.1g; Protein: 4.7g

Ingredients

2 tablespoons olive oil

1 small shallot, chopped

1 carrot, trimmed and chopped

1 parsnip, trimmed and chopped

1 cup yellow squash, peeled and chopped

1 teaspoon fennel seeds

1 teaspoon celery seeds

1 teaspoon turmeric powder

1 bay laurel

1/2 cup amaranth

2 cups cream of celery soup

2 cups water

2 cups collard greens, torn into pieces

Sea salt and ground black pepper, to taste

Directions

In a heavy-bottomed pot, heat the olive oil until sizzling. Once hot, sauté the shallot, carrot, parsnip and squash for 5 minutes or until just tender.

Then, sauté the fennel seeds, celery seeds, turmeric powder and bay laurel for about 30 seconds, until aromatic.

Add in the amaranth, soup and water. Turn the heat to a simmer. Cover and let it simmer for 15 to 18 minutes.

Afterwards, add in the collard greens, season with salt and black pepper and continue to simmer for 5 minutes longer. Enjoy!

Polenta with Mushrooms and Chickpeas

(Ready in about 25 minutes | Servings 4)

Per serving : Calories: 488; Fat: 12.2g; Carbs: 71g; Protein: 21.4g

Ingredients

3 cups vegetable broth

1 cup yellow cornmeal

2 tablespoons olive oil

1 onion, chopped

1 bell pepper, seeded and sliced

1 pound Cremini mushrooms, sliced

2 garlic cloves, minced

1/2 cup dry white wine

1/2 cup vegetable broth

Kosher salt and freshly ground black pepper, to taste

1 teaspoon paprika

1 cup canned chickpeas, drained

Directions

In a medium saucepan, bring the vegetable broth to a boil over medium-high heat. Now, add in the cornmeal, whisking continuously to prevent lumps.

Reduce the heat to a simmer. Continue to simmer, whisking periodically, for about 18 minutes, until the mixture has thickened.

Meanwhile, heat the olive oil in a saucepan over a moderately high heat. Cook the onion and pepper for about 3 minutes or until just tender and fragrant.

Add in the mushrooms and garlic; continue to sauté, gradually adding the wine and broth, for 4 more minutes or until cooked through. Season with salt, black pepper and paprika. Stir in the chickpeas.

Spoon the mushroom mixture over your polenta and serve warm. Bon appétit!

Teff Salad with Avocado and Beans

(Ready in about 20 minutes + chilling time | Servings 2)

Per serving : Calories: 463; Fat: 21.2g; Carbs: 58.9g; Protein: 13.1g

Ingredients

2 cups water

1/2 cup teff grain

1 teaspoon fresh lemon juice

3 tablespoons vegan mayonnaise

1 teaspoon deli mustard

1 small avocado, pitted, peeled and sliced

1 small red onion, thinly sliced

1 small Persian cucumber, sliced

1/2 cup canned kidney beans, drained

2 cups baby spinach

Directions

In a deep saucepan, bring the water to a boil over high heat. Add in the teff grain and turn the heat to a simmer.

Continue to cook, covered, for about 20 minutes or until tender. Let it cool completely.

Add in the remaining ingredients and toss to combine. Serve at room temperature. Bon appétit!

Overnight Oatmeal with Walnuts

(Ready in about 5 minutes + chilling time | Servings 3)

Per serving : Calories: 423; Fat: 16.8g; Carbs: 53.1g; Protein: 17.3g

Ingredients

1 cup old-fashioned oats

3 tablespoons chia seeds

1 ½ cups coconut milk

3 teaspoons agave syrup

1 teaspoon vanilla extract

1/2 teaspoon ground cinnamon

3 tablespoons walnuts, chopped

A pinch of salt

A pinch of grated nutmeg

Directions

Divide the ingredients between three mason jars.

Cover and shake to combine well. Let them sit overnight in your refrigerator.

You can add some extra milk before serving. Enjoy!

Carrot Energy Balls

(Ready in about 10 minutes + chilling time | Servings 8)

Per serving : Calories: 495; Fat: 21.1g; Carbs: 58.4g; Protein: 22.1g

Ingredients

1 large carrot, grated carrot

1 ½ cups old-fashioned oats

1 cup raisins

1 cup dates, pitied

1 cup coconut flakes

1/4 teaspoon ground cloves

1/2 teaspoon ground cinnamon

Directions

In your food processor, pulse all ingredients until it forms a sticky and uniform mixture.

Shape the batter into equal balls.

Place in your refrigerator until ready to serve. Bon appétit!

Crunchy Sweet Potato Bites

(Ready in about 25 minutes + chilling time | Servings 4)

Per serving : Calories: 215; Fat: 4.5g; Carbs: 35g; Protein: 8.7g

Ingredients

4 sweet potatoes, peeled and grated

2 chia eggs

1/4 cup nutritional yeast

2 tablespoons tahini

2 tablespoons chickpea flour

1 teaspoon shallot powder

1 teaspoon garlic powder

1 teaspoon paprika

Sea salt and ground black pepper, to taste

Directions

Start by preheating your oven to 395 degrees F. Line a baking pan with parchment paper or Silpat mat.

Thoroughly combine all the ingredients until everything is well incorporated.

Roll the batter into equal balls and place them in your refrigerator for about 1 hour.

Bake these balls for approximately 25 minutes, turning them over halfway through the cooking time. Bon appétit!

Roasted Glazed Baby Carrots

(Ready in about 30 minutes | Servings 6)

Per serving : Calories: 165; Fat: 10.1g; Carbs: 16.5g; Protein: 1.4g

Ingredients

2 pounds baby carrots

1/4 cup olive oil

1/4 cup apple cider vinegar

1/2 teaspoon red pepper flakes

Sea salt and freshly ground black pepper, to taste

1 tablespoon agave syrup

2 tablespoons soy sauce

1 tablespoon fresh cilantro, minced

Directions

Start by preheating your oven 395 degrees F.

Then, toss the carrots with the olive oil, vinegar, red pepper, salt, black pepper, agave syrup and soy sauce.

Roast the carrots for about 30 minutes, rotating the pan once or twice. Garnish with fresh cilantro and serve. Bon appétit!

Oven-Baked Kale Chips

(Ready in about 20 minutes | Servings 8)

Per serving : Calories: 65; Fat: 3.9g; Carbs: 5.3g; Protein: 2.4g

Ingredients

2 bunches kale, leaves separated

2 tablespoons olive oil

1/2 teaspoon mustard seeds

1/2 teaspoon celery seeds

1/2 teaspoon dried oregano

1/4 teaspoon ground cumin

1 teaspoon garlic powder

Coarse sea salt and ground black pepper, to taste

Directions

Start by preheating your oven to 340 degrees F. Line a baking sheet with parchment paper or Silpat mar.

Toss the kale leaves with the remaining ingredients until well coated.

Bake in the preheated oven for about 13 minutes, rotating the pan once or twice. Bon appétit!

Cheesy Cashew Dip

(Ready in about 10 minutes | Servings 8)

Per serving : Calories: 115; Fat: 8.6g; Carbs: 6.6g; Protein: 4.4g

Ingredients

1 cup raw cashews

1 lemon, freshly squeezed

2 tablespoons tahini

2 tablespoons nutritional yeast

1/2 teaspoon turmeric powder

1/2 teaspoon red pepper flakes, crushed

Sea salt and ground black pepper, to taste

Directions

Place all the ingredients in the bowl of your food processor. Blend until uniform, creamy and smooth. You can add a splash of water to thin it out, as needed.

Spoon your dip into a serving bowl; serve with veggie sticks, chips, or crackers.

Bon appétit!

Peppery Hummus Dip

(Ready in about 10 minutes | Servings 10)

Per serving : Calories: 155; Fat: 7.9g; Carbs: 17.4g; Protein: 5.9g

Ingredients

20 ounces canned or boiled chickpeas, drained

1/4 cup tahini

2 garlic cloves, minced

2 tablespoons lemon juice, freshly squeezed

1/2 cup chickpea liquid

2 red roasted peppers, seeded and sliced

1/2 teaspoon paprika

1 teaspoon dried basil

Sea salt and ground black pepper, to taste

2 tablespoons olive oil

Directions

Blitz all the ingredients, except for the oil, in your blender or food processor until your desired consistency is reached.

Place in your refrigerator until ready to serve.

Serve with toasted pita wedges or chips, if desired. Bon appétit!

Traditional Lebanese Mutabal

(Ready in about 10 minutes | Servings 6)

Per serving : Calories: 115; Fat: 7.8g; Carbs: 9.8g; Protein: 2.9g

Ingredients

1 pound eggplant

1 onion, chopped

1 tablespoon garlic paste

4 tablespoons tahini

1 tablespoon coconut oil

2 tablespoons lemon juice

1/2 teaspoon ground coriander

1/4 cup ground cloves

1 teaspoon red pepper flakes

1 teaspoon smoked peppers

Sea salt and ground black pepper, to taste

Directions

Roast the eggplant until the skin turns black; peel the eggplant and transfer it to the bowl of your food processor.

Add in the remaining ingredients. Blend until everything is well incorporated.

Serve with crostini or pita bread, if desired. Bon appétit!

Indian-Style Roasted Chickpeas

(Ready in about 10 minutes | Servings 8)

Per serving : Calories: 223; Fat: 6.4g; Carbs: 32.2g; Protein: 10.4g

Ingredients

2 cups canned chickpeas, drained

2 tablespoons olive oil

1/2 teaspoon garlic powder

1/2 teaspoon paprika

1 teaspoon curry powder

1 teaspoon garam masala

Sea salt and red pepper, to taste

Directions

Pat the chickpeas dry using paper towels. Drizzle olive oil over the chickpeas.

Roast the chickpeas in the preheated oven at 400 degrees F for about 25 minutes, tossing them once or twice.

Toss your chickpeas with the spices and enjoy!

Avocado with Tahini Sauce

(Ready in about 10 minutes | Servings 4)

Per serving : Calories: 304; Fat: 25.7g; Carbs: 17.6g; Protein: 6g

Ingredients

2 large-sized avocados, pitted and halved

4 tablespoons tahini

4 tablespoons soy sauce

1 tablespoon lemon juice

1/2 teaspoon red pepper flakes

Sea salt and ground black pepper, to taste

1 teaspoon garlic powder

Directions

Place the avocado halves on a serving platter.

Mix the tahini, soy sauce, lemon juice, red pepper, salt, black pepper and garlic powder in a small bowl. Divide the sauce between the avocado halves.

Bon appétit!

Sweet Potato Tater Tots

(Ready in about 25 minutes + chilling time | Servings 4)

Per serving : Calories: 232; Fat: 7.1g; Carbs: 37g; Protein: 8.4g

Ingredients

1 ½ pounds sweet potatoes, grated

2 chia eggs

1/2 cup plain flour

1/2 cup breadcrumbs

3 tablespoons hummus

Sea salt and black pepper, to taste

1 tablespoon olive oil

1/2 cup salsa sauce

Directions

Start by preheating your oven to 395 degrees F. Line a baking pan with parchment paper or Silpat mat.

Thoroughly combine all the ingredients, except for the salsa, until everything is well incorporated.

Roll the batter into equal balls and place them in your refrigerator for about 1 hour.

Bake these balls for approximately 25 minutes, turning them over halfway through the cooking time. Bon appétit!

Roasted Pepper and Tomato Dip

(Ready in about 35 minutes | Servings 10)

Per serving : Calories: 90; Fat: 5.7g; Carbs: 8.5g; Protein: 1.9g

Ingredients

4 red bell peppers

4 tomatoes

4 tablespoons olive oil

1 red onion, chopped

4 garlic cloves

4 ounces canned garbanzo beans, drained

Sea salt and ground black pepper, to taste

Directions

Start by preheating your oven to 400 degrees F.

Place the peppers and tomatoes on a parchment-lined baking pan. Bake for about 30 minutes; peel the peppers and transfer them to your food processor along with the roasted tomatoes.

Meanwhile, heat 2 tablespoons of the olive oil in a frying pan over medium-high heat. Sauté the onion and garlic for about 5 minutes or until they've softened.

Add the sautéed vegetables to your food processor. Add in the garbanzo beans, salt, pepper and the remaining olive oil; process until creamy and smooth.

Bon appétit!

Classic Party Mix

(Ready in about 1 hour 5 minutes | Servings 15)

Per serving : Calories: 290; Fat: 12.2g; Carbs: 39g; Protein: 7.5g

Ingredients

5 cups vegan corn cereal

3 cups vegan mini pretzels

1 cup almonds, roasted

1/2 cup pepitas, toasted

1 tablespoon nutritional yeast

1 tablespoon balsamic vinegar

1 tablespoon soy sauce

1 teaspoon garlic powder

1/3 cup vegan butter

Directions

Start by preheating your oven to 250 degrees F. Line a large baking pan with parchment paper or Silpat mat.

Mix the cereal, pretzels, almonds and pepitas in a serving bowl.

In a small saucepan, melt the remaining ingredients over a moderate heat. Pour the sauce over the cereal/nut mixture.

Bake for about 1 hour, stirring every 15 minutes, until golden and fragrant. Transfer it to a wire rack to cool completely. Bon appétit!

Olive Oil Garlic Crostini

(Ready in about 10 minutes | Servings 4)

Per serving : Calories: 289; Fat: 8.2g; Carbs: 44.9g; Protein: 9.5g

Ingredients

- 1 whole-grain baguette, sliced
- 4 tablespoons extra-virgin olive oil
- 1/2 teaspoon sea salt
- 3 cloves garlic, halved

Directions

Preheat your broiler.

Brush each slice of bread with the olive oil and sprinkle with sea salt. Place under the preheated broiler for about 2 minutes or until lightly toasted.

Rub each slice of bread with the garlic and serve. Bon appétit!

Classic Vegan Meatballs

(Ready in about 15 minutes | Servings 4)

Per serving : Calories: 159; Fat: 9.2g; Carbs: 16.3g; Protein: 2.9g

Ingredients

1 cup brown rice, cooked and cooled

1 cup canned or boiled red kidney beans, drained

1 teaspoon fresh garlic, minced

1 small onion, chopped

Sea salt and ground black pepper, to taste

1/2 teaspoon cayenne pepper

1/2 teaspoon smoked paprika

1/2 teaspoon coriander seeds

1/2 teaspoon coriander mustard seeds

2 tablespoons olive oil

Directions

In a mixing bowl, thoroughly combine all the ingredients, except for the olive oil. Mix to combine well and then, shape the mixture into equal balls using oiled hands.

Then, heat the olive oil in a nonstick skillet over medium heat. Once hot, fry the meatballs for about 10 minutes until golden brown on all sides.

Serve with cocktail sticks and enjoy!

Balsamic Roasted Parsnip

(Ready in about 30 minutes | Servings 6)

Per serving : Calories: 174; Fat: 9.3g; Carbs: 22.2g; Protein: 1.4g

Ingredients

1 ½ pounds parsnips, cut into sticks

1/4 cup olive oil

1/4 cup balsamic vinegar

1 teaspoon Dijon mustard

1 teaspoon fennel seeds

Sea salt and ground black pepper, to taste

1 teaspoon Mediterranean spice mix

Directions

Toss all ingredients in a mixing bowl until the parsnips are well coated.

Roast the parsnip in the preheated oven at 400 degrees F for about 30 minutes, stirring halfway through the cooking time.

Serve at room temperature and enjoy!

Traditional Baba Ganoush

(Ready in about 25 minutes | Servings 8)

Per serving : Calories: 104; Fat: 8.2g; Carbs: 5.3g; Protein: 1.6g

Ingredients

1 pound eggplant, cut into rounds

1 teaspoon coarse sea salt

3 tablespoons olive oil

3 tablespoons fresh lime juice

2 cloves garlic, minced

3 tablespoons tahini

1/4 teaspoon ground cloves

1/2 teaspoon ground cumin

2 tablespoons fresh parsley, roughly chopped

Directions

Rub the sea salt all over the eggplant rounds. Then, place them in a colander and let it sit for about 15 minutes; drain, rinse and pat dry with kitchen towels.

Roast the eggplant until the skin turns black; peel the eggplant and transfer it to the bowl of your food processor.

Add in the olive oil, lime juice, garlic, tahini, cloves and cumin. Blend until everything is well incorporated.

Garnish with fresh parsley leaves and enjoy!

Peanut Butter Date Bites

(Ready in about 5 minutes | Servings 2)

Per serving : Calories: 143; Fat: 3.9g; Carbs: 26.3g; Protein: 2.6g

Ingredients

8 fresh dates, pitted and cut into halves

8 teaspoons peanut butter

1/4 teaspoon ground cinnamon

Directions

Divide the peanut butter between the date halves.

Dust with cinnamon and serve immediately. Bon appétit!

Roasted Cauliflower Dip

(Ready in about 30 minutes | Servings 7)

Per serving : Calories: 142; Fat: 12.5g; Carbs: 6.3g; Protein: 2.9g

Ingredients

1 pound cauliflower florets

1/4 cup olive oil

4 tablespoons tahini

1/2 teaspoon paprika

Sea salt and ground black pepper, to taste

2 tablespoons fresh lime juice

2 cloves garlic, minced

Directions

Start by preheating your oven to 420 degrees F. Toss the cauliflower florets with the olive oil and arrange them on a parchment-lined baking pan.

Bake for about 25 minutes or until tender.

Then, puree the cauliflower along with the remaining ingredients, adding cooking liquid, as needed.

Drizzle with some extra olive oil, if desired. Bon appétit!

Easy Zucchini Roll-Ups

(Ready in about 10 minutes | Servings 5)

Per serving : Calories: 99; Fat: 4.4g; Carbs: 12.1g; Protein: 3.1g

Ingredients

1 cup hummus, preferably homemade

1 medium tomato, chopped

1 teaspoon mustard

1/4 teaspoon oregano

1/2 teaspoon cayenne pepper

Sea salt and ground black pepper, to taste

1 large zucchini, cut into strips

2 tablespoons fresh basil, chopped

2 tablespoons fresh parsley, chopped

Directions

In a mixing bowl, thoroughly combine the hummus, tomato, mustard, oregano, cayenne pepper, salt and black pepper.

Divide the filling between the zucchini strips and spread it out evenly. Roll the zucchini up and garnish with fresh basil and parsley.

Bon appétit!

Chipotle Sweet Potato Fries

(Ready in about 45 minutes | Servings 4)

Per serving : Calories: 186; Fat: 7.1g; Carbs: 29.6g; Protein: 2.5g

Ingredients

- 4 medium sweet potatoes, peeled and cut into sticks
- 2 tablespoons peanut oil
- Sea salt and ground black pepper, to taste
- 1 teaspoon chipotle pepper powder
- 1/4 teaspoon ground allspice
- 1 teaspoon brown sugar
- 1 teaspoon dried rosemary

Directions

Toss the sweet potato fries with the remaining ingredients.

Bake your fries at 375 degrees F for about 45 minutes or until browned; make sure to stir the fries once or twice.

Serve with your favorite dipping sauce, if desired. Bon appétit!

Cannellini Bean Dipping Sauce

(Ready in about 10 minutes | Servings 6)

Per serving : Calories: 123; Fat: 4.5g; Carbs: 15.6g; Protein: 5.6g

Ingredients

10 ounces canned cannellini beans, drained

1 clove garlic, minced

2 roasted peppers, sliced

Sea freshly ground black pepper, to taste

1/2 teaspoon ground cumin

1/2 teaspoon mustard seeds

1/2 teaspoon ground bay leaves

3 tablespoons tahini

2 tablespoons fresh Italian parsley, chopped

Directions

Place all the ingredients, except for the parsley, in the bowl of your blender or food processor. Blitz until well blended.

Transfer the sauce to a serving bowl and garnish with fresh parsley.

Serve with pita wedges, tortilla chips, or veggie sticks, if desired. Enjoy!

Spiced Roasted Cauliflower

(Ready in about 25 minutes | Servings 6)

Per serving : Calories: 115; Fat: 9.3g; Carbs: 6.9g; Protein: 5.6g

Ingredients

1 ½ pounds cauliflower florets

1/4 cup olive oil

4 tablespoons apple cider vinegar

2 cloves garlic, pressed

1 teaspoon dried basil

1 teaspoon dried oregano

Sea salt and ground black pepper, to taste

Directions

Begin by preheating your oven to 420 degrees F.

Toss the cauliflower florets with the remaining ingredients.

Arrange the cauliflower florets on a parchment-lined baking sheet. Bake the cauliflower florets in the preheated oven for about 25 minutes or until they are slightly charred.

Bon appétit!

Easy Lebanese Toum

(Ready in about 10 minutes | Servings 6)

Per serving : Calories: 252; Fat: 27g; Carbs: 3.1g; Protein: 0.4g

Ingredients

2 heads garlic

1 teaspoon coarse sea salt

1 ½ cups olive oil

1 lemon, freshly squeezed

2 cups carrots, cut into matchsticks

Directions

Puree the garlic cloves and salt in your food processor of a high-speed blender until creamy and smooth, scraping down the sides of the bowl.

Gradually and slowly, add in the olive oil and lemon juice, alternating between these two ingredients to create a fluffy sauce.

Blend until the sauce has thickened. Serve with carrot sticks and enjoy!

Avocado with Tangy Ginger Dressing

(Ready in about 10 minutes | Servings 4)

Per serving : Calories: 295; Fat: 28.2g; Carbs: 11.3g; Protein: 2.3g

Ingredients

2 avocados, pitted and halved

1 clove garlic, pressed

1 teaspoon fresh ginger, peeled and minced

2 tablespoons balsamic vinegar

4 tablespoons extra-virgin olive oil

Kosher salt and ground black pepper, to taste

Directions

Place the avocado halves on a serving platter.

Mix the garlic, ginger, vinegar, olive oil, salt and black pepper in a small bowl. Divide the sauce between the avocado halves.

Bon appétit!

Chickpea Snack Mix

(Ready in about 30 minutes | Servings 8)

Per serving : Calories: 109; Fat: 7.9g; Carbs: 7.4g; Protein: 3.4g

Ingredients

1 cup roasted chickpeas, drained

2 tablespoons coconut oil, melted

1/4 cup raw pumpkin seeds

1/4 cup raw pecan halves

1/3 cup dried cherries

Directions

Pat the chickpeas dry using paper towels. Drizzle coconut oil over the chickpeas.

Roast the chickpeas in the preheated oven at 380 degrees F for about 20 minutes, tossing them once or twice.

Toss your chickpeas with the pumpkin seeds and pecan halves. Continue baking until the nuts are fragrant about 8 minutes; let cool completely.

Add in the dried cherries and stir to combine. Bon appétit!

Muhammara Dip with a Twist

(Ready in about 35 minutes / Servings 9)

Per serving : Calories: 149; Fat: 11.5g; Carbs: 8.9g; Protein: 2.4g

Ingredients

3 red bell peppers

5 tablespoons olive oil

2 garlic cloves, chopped

1 tomato, chopped

3/4 cup bread crumbs

2 tablespoons molasses

1 teaspoon ground cumin

1/4 sunflower seeds, toasted

1 Maras pepper, minced

2 tablespoons tahini

Sea salt and red pepper, to taste

Directions

Start by preheating your oven to 400 degrees F.

Place the peppers on a parchment-lined baking pan. Bake for about 30 minutes; peel the peppers and transfer them to your food processor.

Meanwhile, heat 2 tablespoons of the olive oil in a frying pan over medium-high heat. Sauté the garlic and tomatoes for about 5 minutes or until they've softened.

Add the sautéed vegetables to your food processor. Add in the remaining ingredients and process until creamy and smooth.

Bon appétit!

Spinach, Chickpea and Garlic Crostini

(Ready in about 10 minutes | Servings 6)

Per serving : Calories: 242; Fat: 6.1g; Carbs: 38.5g; Protein: 8.9g

Ingredients

1 baguette, cut into slices

4 tablespoons extra-virgin olive oil

Sea salt and red pepper, to season

3 garlic cloves, minced

1 cup boiled chickpeas, drained

2 cups spinach

1 tablespoon fresh lemon juice

Directions

Preheat your broiler.

Brush the slices of bread with 2 tablespoons of the olive oil and sprinkle with sea salt and red pepper. Place under the preheated broiler for about 2 minutes or until lightly toasted.

In a mixing bowl, thoroughly combine the garlic, chickpeas, spinach, lemon juice and the remaining 2 tablespoons of the olive oil.

Spoon the chickpea mixture onto each toast. Bon appétit!

Mushroom and Cannellini Bean "Meatballs"

(Ready in about 15 minutes | Servings 4)

Per serving : Calories: 195; Fat: 14.1g; Carbs: 13.2g; Protein: 3.9g

Ingredients

4 tablespoons olive oil

1 cup button mushrooms, chopped

1 shallot, chopped

2 garlic cloves, crushed

1 cup canned or boiled cannellini beans, drained

1 cup quinoa, cooked

Sea salt and ground black pepper, to taste

1 teaspoon smoked paprika

1/2 teaspoon red pepper flakes

1 teaspoon mustard seeds

1/2 teaspoon dried dill

Directions

Heat 2 tablespoons of the olive oil in a nonstick skillet. Once hot, cook the mushrooms and shallot for 3 minutes or until just tender.

Add in the garlic, beans, quinoa and spices. Mix to combine well and then, shape the mixture into equal balls using oiled hands.

Then, heat the remaining 2 tablespoons of the olive oil in a nonstick skillet over medium heat. Once hot, fry the meatballs for about 10 minutes until golden brown on all sides.

Serve with cocktail sticks. Bon appétit!

Cucumber Rounds with Hummus

(Ready in about 10 minutes | Servings 6)

Per serving : Calories: 88; Fat: 3.6g; Carbs: 11.3g; Protein: 2.6g

Ingredients

1 cup hummus, preferably homemade

2 large tomatoes, diced

1/2 teaspoon red pepper flakes

Sea salt and ground black pepper, to taste

2 English cucumbers, sliced into rounds

Directions

Divide the hummus dip between the cucumber rounds.

Top them with tomatoes; sprinkle red pepper flakes, salt and black pepper over each cucumber.

Serve well chilled and enjoy!

Stuffed Jalapeño Bites

(Ready in about 15 minutes | Servings 6)

Per serving : Calories: 108; Fat: 6.6g; Carbs: 7.3g; Protein: 5.3g

Ingredients

1/2 cup raw sunflower seeds, soaked overnight and drained

4 tablespoons scallions, chopped

1 teaspoon garlic, minced

3 tablespoons nutritional yeast

1/2 cup cream of onion soup

1/2 teaspoon cayenne pepper

1/2 teaspoon mustard seeds

12 jalapeños, halved and seeded

1/2 cup breadcrumbs

Directions

In your food processor or high-speed blender, blitz raw sunflower seeds, scallions, garlic, nutritional yeast, soup, cayenne pepper and mustard seeds until well combined.

Spoon the mixture into the jalapeños and top them with the breadcrumbs.

Bake in the preheated oven at 400 degrees F for about 13 minutes or until the peppers have softened. Serve warm.

Bon appétit!

Mexican-Style Onion Rings

(Ready in about 35 minutes | Servings 6)

Per serving : Calories: 213; Fat: 10.6g; Carbs: 26.2g; Protein: 4.3g

Ingredients

2 medium onions, cut into rings

1/4 cup all-purpose flour

1/4 cup spelt flour

1/3 cup rice milk, unsweetened

1/3 cup ale beer

Sea salt and ground black pepper, to season

1/2 teaspoon cayenne pepper

1/2 teaspoon mustard seeds

1 cup tortilla chips, crushed

1 tablespoon olive oil

Directions

Start by preheating your oven to 420 degrees F.

In a shallow bowl, mix the flour, milk and beer.

In another shallow bowl, mix the spices with the crushed tortilla chips. Dredge the onion rings in the flour mixture.

Then, roll them over the spiced mixture, pressing down to coat well.

Arrange the onion rings on a parchment-lined baking pan. Brush them with olive oil and bake for approximately 30 minutes. Bon appétit!

Roasted Root Vegetables

(Ready in about 35 minutes | Servings 6)

Per serving : Calories: 261; Fat: 18.2g; Carbs: 23.3g; Protein: 2.3g

Ingredients

1/4 cup olive oil

2 carrots, peeled and cut into 1 ½-inch pieces

2 parsnips, peeled and cut into 1 ½-inch pieces

1 celery stalk, peeled and cut into 1 ½-inch pieces

1 pound sweet potatoes, peeled and cut into 1 ½-inch pieces

1/4 cup olive oil

1 teaspoon mustard seeds

1/2 teaspoon basil

1/2 teaspoon oregano

1 teaspoon red pepper flakes

1 teaspoon dried thyme

Sea salt and ground black pepper, to taste

Directions

Toss the vegetables with the remaining ingredients until well coated.

Roast the vegetables in the preheated oven at 400 degrees F for about 35 minutes, stirring halfway through the cooking time.

Taste, adjust the seasonings and serve warm. Bon appétit!

Indian-Style Hummus Dip

(Ready in about 10 minutes | Servings 10)

Per serving : Calories: 171; Fat: 10.4g; Carbs: 15.3g; Protein: 5.4g

Ingredients

- 20 ounces canned or boiled chickpeas, drained
- 1 teaspoon garlic, sliced
- 1/4 cup tahini
- 1/4 cup olive oil
- 1 lime, freshly squeezed
- 1/4 teaspoon turmeric
- 1/2 teaspoon cumin powder
- 1 teaspoon curry powder
- 1 teaspoon coriander seeds
- 1/4 cup chickpea liquid, or more, as needed
- 2 tablespoons fresh cilantro, roughly chopped

Directions

Blitz the chickpeas, garlic, tahini, olive oil, lime, turmeric, cumin, curry powder and coriander seeds in your blender or food processor.

Blend until your desired consistency is reached, gradually adding the chickpea liquid.

Place in your refrigerator until ready to serve. Garnish with fresh cilantro.

Serve with naan bread or veggie sticks, if desired. Bon appétit!

Roasted Carrot and Bean Dip

(Ready in about 55 minutes | Servings 10)

Per serving : Calories: 121; Fat: 8.3g; Carbs: 11.2g; Protein: 2.8g

Ingredients

1 ½ pounds carrots, trimmed

2 tablespoons olive oil

4 tablespoons tahini

8 ounces canned cannellini beans, drained

1 teaspoon garlic, chopped

2 tablespoons lemon juice

2 tablespoons soy sauce

Sea salt and ground black pepper, to taste

1/2 teaspoon paprika

1/2 teaspoon dried dill

1/4 cup pepitas, toasted

Directions

Begin by preheating your oven to 390 degrees F. Line a roasting pan with parchment paper.

Now, toss the carrots with the olive oil and arrange them on the prepared roasting pan.

Roast the carrots for about 50 minutes or until tender. Transfer the roasted carrots to the bowl of your food processor.

Add in the tahini, beans, garlic, lemon juice, soy sauce, salt, black pepper, paprika and dill. Process until your dip is creamy and uniform.

Garnish with toasted pepitas and serve with dippers of choice. Bon appétit!

Quick and Easy Zucchini Sushi

(Ready in about 10 minutes | Servings 5)

Per serving : Calories: 129; Fat: 6.3g; Carbs: 15.9g; Protein: 2.5g

Ingredients

1 cup rice, cooked

1 carrot, grated

1 small onion, grated

1 avocado, chopped

1 garlic clove, minced

Sea salt and ground black pepper, to taste

1 medium zucchini, cut into strips

Wasabi sauce, to serve

Directions

In a mixing bowl, thoroughly combine the rice, carrot, onion, avocado, garlic, salt and black pepper.

Divide the filling between the zucchini strips and spread it out evenly. Roll the zucchini up and serve with Wasabi sauce.

Bon appétit!

Cherry Tomatoes with Hummus

(Ready in about 10 minutes | Servings 8)

Per serving : Calories: 49; Fat: 2.5g; Carbs: 4.7g; Protein: 1.3g

Ingredients

- 1/2 cup hummus, preferably homemade
- 2 tablespoons vegan mayonnaise
- 1/4 cup scallions, chopped
- 16 cherry tomatoes, scoop out pulp
- 2 tablespoons fresh cilantro, chopped

Directions

In a mixing bowl, thoroughly combine the hummus, mayonnaise and scallions.

Divide the hummus mixture between the tomatoes. Garnish with fresh cilantro and serve.

Bon appétit!

Oven-Roasted Button Mushrooms

(Ready in about 20 minutes | Servings 4)

Per serving : Calories: 136; Fat: 10.5g; Carbs: 7.6g; Protein: 5.6g

Ingredients

1 ½ pounds button mushrooms, cleaned

3 tablespoons olive oil

3 garlic cloves, minced

1 teaspoon dried oregano

1 teaspoon dried basil

1/2 teaspoon dried rosemary

Kosher salt and ground black pepper, to taste

Directions

Toss the mushrooms with the remaining ingredients.

Arrange the mushrooms on a parchment-lined roasting pan.

Bake the mushrooms in the preheated oven at 420 degrees F for about 20 minutes or until tender and fragrant.

Arrange the mushrooms on a serving platter and serve with cocktail sticks. Bon appétit!

Cheesy Kale Chips

(Ready in about 1 hour 30 minutes | Servings 6)

Per serving : Calories: 121; Fat: 7.5g; Carbs: 8.4g; Protein: 6.5g

Ingredients

1/2 cup sunflower seeds, soaked overnight and drained

1/2 cup cashews, soaked overnight and drained

1/3 cup nutritional yeast

2 tablespoons lemon juice

1 teaspoon onion powder

1 teaspoon garlic powder

1 teaspoon paprika

Sea salt and ground black pepper, to taste

1/2 cup water

4 cups kale, torn into pieces

Directions

In your food processor or high-speed blender, blitz the raw sunflower seeds, cashews, nutritional yeast, lemon juice, onion powder, garlic powder, paprika, salt, ground black pepper and water until well combined.

Pour the mixture over the kale leaves and mix until they are well coated.

Bake in the preheated oven at 220 degrees F for about 1 hour 30 minutes or until crispy.

Bon appétit!

Hummus Avocado Boats

(Ready in about 10 minutes | Servings 4)

Per serving : Calories: 297; Fat: 21.2g; Carbs: 23.9g; Protein: 6g

Ingredients

1 tablespoon fresh lemon juice

2 ripe avocados, halved and pitted

8 ounces hummus

1 garlic clove, minced

1 medium tomato, chopped

Sea salt and ground black pepper, to taste

1/2 teaspoon turmeric powder

1/2 teaspoon cayenne pepper

1 tablespoon tahini

Directions

Drizzle the fresh lemon juice over the avocado halves.

Mix the hummus, garlic, tomato, salt, black pepper, turmeric powder, cayenne pepper and tahini. Spoon the filling into your avocados.

Serve immediately.

Nacho Stuffed Button Mushrooms

(Ready in about 25 minutes | Servings 5)

Per serving : Calories: 210; Fat: 13.4g; Carbs: 17.7g; Protein: 6.9g

Ingredients

1 cup tortilla chips, crushed

1 cup canned or cooked black beans, drained

4 tablespoons vegan butter

2 tablespoons tahini

4 tablespoons scallions, chopped

1 teaspoon garlic, minced

1 jalapeno, chopped

1 teaspoon Mexican oregano

1 teaspoon cayenne pepper

Sea salt and ground black pepper, to taste

15 medium button mushrooms, cleaned, stalks removed

Directions

Thoroughly combine all the ingredients, except for the mushrooms, in a mixing bowl.

Divide the nacho mixture between your mushrooms.

Bake in the preheated oven at 350 degrees F for about 20 minutes or until tender and cooked through. Bon appétit!

Lettuce Wraps with Hummus and Avocado

(Ready in about 10 minutes | Servings 6)

Per serving : Calories: 115; Fat: 6.9g; Carbs: 11.6g; Protein: 2.6g

Ingredients

1/2 cup hummus

1 tomato, chopped

1 carrot, shredded

1 medium avocado, pitted and diced

1 teaspoon white vinegar

1 teaspoon soy sauce

1 teaspoon agave syrup

1 tablespoon Sriracha sauce

1 teaspoon garlic, minced

1 teaspoon ginger, freshly grated

Kosher salt and ground black pepper, to taste

1 head butter lettuce, separated into leaves

Directions

Thoroughly combine the hummus, tomato, carrot and avocado. Combine the white vinegar, soy sauce, agave syrup, Sriracha sauce, garlic, ginger, salt and black pepper.

Divide the filling between lettuce leaves, roll them up and serve with sauce on the side.

Bon appétit!

Roasted Brussels Sprouts

(Ready in about 35 minutes | Servings 6)

Per serving : Calories: 151; Fat: 9.6g; Carbs: 14.5g; Protein: 5.3g

Ingredients

2 pounds Brussels sprouts

1/4 cup olive oil

Coarse sea salt and ground black pepper, to taste

1 teaspoon red pepper flakes

1 teaspoon dried oregano

1 teaspoon dried parsley

1 teaspoon mustard seeds

Directions

Toss the Brussels sprouts with the remaining ingredients until well coated.

Roast the vegetables in the preheated oven at 400 degrees F for about 35 minutes, stirring halfway through the cooking time.

Taste, adjust the seasonings and serve warm. Bon appétit!

Sweet Potato Poblano Poppers

(Ready in about 25 minutes | Servings 7)

Per serving : Calories: 145; Fat: 3.6g; Carbs: 24.9g; Protein: 5.3g

Ingredients

1/2 pound cauliflower, trimmed and diced

1 pound sweet potatoes, peeled and diced

1/2 cup cashew milk, unsweetened

1/4 cup vegan mayonnaise

1/2 teaspoon curry powder

1/2 teaspoon cayenne pepper

1/4 teaspoon dried dill

Sea and ground black pepper, to taste

1/2 cup fresh breadcrumbs

14 fresh poblano chiles, cut into halves, seeds removed

Directions

Steam the cauliflower and sweet potatoes for about 10 minutes or until they've softened. Now, mash them with the cashew milk.

Add in the vegan mayo, curry powder, cayenne pepper, dill, salt and black pepper.

Spoon the mixture into the peppers and top them with the breadcrumbs.

Bake in the preheated oven at 400 degrees F for about 13 minutes or until the peppers have softened.

Bon appétit!

Baked Zucchini Chips

(Ready in about 1 hour 30 minutes | Servings 7)

Per serving : Calories: 48; Fat: 4.2g; Carbs: 2g; Protein: 1.7g

Ingredients

1 pound zucchini, cut into 1/8-inch thick slices

2 tablespoons olive oil

1/2 teaspoon dried oregano

1/2 teaspoon dried basil

1/2 teaspoon red pepper flakes

Sea salt and ground black pepper, to taste

Directions

Toss the zucchini with the remaining ingredients.

Lay the zucchini slices in a single layer on a parchment-lined baking pan.

Bake at 235 degrees F for about 90 minutes until crisp and golden. Zucchini chips will crisp up as it cools.

Bon appétit!

Authentic Lebanese Dip

(Ready in about 10 minutes | Servings 12)

Per serving : Calories: 117; Fat: 6.6g; Carbs: 12.2g; Protein: 4.3g

Ingredients

2 (15-ounce) can chickpeas/garbanzo beans

4 tablespoons lemon juice

4 tablespoons tahini

2 tablespoons olive oil

1 teaspoon ginger-garlic paste

1 teaspoon Lebanese 7 spice blend

Sea salt and ground black pepper, to taste

1/3 cup chickpea liquid

Directions

Blitz the chickpeas, lemon juice, tahini, olive oil, ginger-garlic paste and spices in your blender or food processor.

Blend until your desired consistency is reached, gradually adding the chickpea liquid.

Place in your refrigerator until ready to serve. Serve with veggie sticks, if desired. Bon appétit!

Oat Vegan Meatballs

(Ready in about 15 minutes | Servings 4)

Per serving : Calories: 284; Fat: 10.5g; Carbs: 38.2g; Protein: 10.4g

Ingredients

1 cup rolled oats

1 cup boiled or canned chickpeas

2 cloves garlic, minced

1 teaspoon onion powder

1/2 teaspoon cumin powder

1 teaspoon dried parsley flakes

1 teaspoon dried marjoram

1 tablespoon chia seeds, soaked with 2 tablespoons of water

A few drizzles liquid smoke

Sea salt and freshly ground black pepper, to taste

2 tablespoons olive oil

Directions

Thoroughly combine the ingredients, except for the olive oil. Mix to combine well and then, shape the mixture into equal balls using oiled hands.

Then, heat the olive oil in a nonstick skillet over medium heat. Once hot, fry the meatballs for about 10 minutes until golden brown on all sides.

Arrange your meatballs on a serving platter and serve with cocktail sticks. Bon appétit!

Bell Pepper Boats with Mango Salsa

(Ready in about 5 minutes | Servings 4)

Per serving : Calories: 74; Fat: 0.5g; Carbs: 17.6g; Protein: 1.6g

Ingredients

1 mango, peeled, pitted, cubed

1 small shallot, chopped

2 tablespoons fresh cilantro, minced

1 red chile pepper, seeded and chopped

1 tablespoon fresh lime juice

4 bell peppers, seeded and halved

Directions

Thoroughly combine the mango, shallot, cilantro, red chile pepper and lime juice.

Spoon the mixture into the pepper halves and serve immediately.

Bon appétit!

Tangy Rosemary Broccoli Florets

(Ready in about 35 minutes | Servings 6)

Per serving : Calories: 135; Fat: 9.5g; Carbs: 10.9g; Protein: 4.4g

Ingredients

2 pounds broccoli florets

1/4 cup extra-virgin olive oil

Sea salt and ground black pepper, to taste

1 teaspoon ginger-garlic paste

1 tablespoon fresh rosemary, chopped

1/2 teaspoon lemon zest

Directions

Toss the broccoli with the remaining ingredients until well coated.

Roast the vegetables in the preheated oven at 400 degrees F for about 35 minutes, stirring halfway through the cooking time.

Taste, adjust the seasonings and serve warm. Bon appétit!

Crispy Baked Beetroot Chips

(Ready in about 35 minutes | Servings 6)

Per serving : Calories: 92; Fat: 9.1g; Carbs: 2.6g; Protein: 0.5g

Ingredients

2 red beetroots, peeled and cut into 1/8-inch-thick slices

1/4 cup olive oil

Sea salt and ground black pepper, to taste

1/2 teaspoon red pepper flakes

Directions

Toss the beetroot slices with the remaining ingredients.

Arrange the beetroot slices in a single layer on a parchment-lined baking pan.

Bake at 400 degrees F for about 30 minutes until crisp. Bon appétit!

Red Kidney Bean Salad

(Ready in about 1 hour + chilling time | Servings 6)

Per serving : Calories: 443; Fat: 19.2g; Carbs: 52.2g; Protein: 18.1g

Ingredients

3/4 pound red kidney beans, soaked overnight

2 bell peppers, chopped

1 carrot, trimmed and grated

3 ounces frozen or canned corn kernels, drained

3 heaping tablespoons scallions, chopped

2 cloves garlic, minced

1 red chile pepper, sliced

1/2 cup extra-virgin olive oil

2 tablespoons apple cider vinegar

2 tablespoons fresh lemon juice

Sea salt and ground black pepper, to taste

2 tablespoons fresh cilantro, chopped

2 tablespoons fresh parsley, chopped

2 tablespoons fresh basil, chopped

Directions

Cover the soaked beans with a fresh change of cold water and bring to a boil. Let it boil for about 10 minutes. Turn the heat to a simmer and continue to cook for 50 to 55 minutes or until tender.

Allow your beans to cool completely, then, transfer them to a salad bowl.

Add in the remaining ingredients and toss to combine well. Bon appétit!

Anasazi Bean and Vegetable Stew

(Ready in about 1 hour | Servings 3)

Per serving : Calories: 444; Fat: 15.8g; Carbs: 58.2g; Protein: 20.2g

Ingredients

1 cup Anasazi beans, soaked overnight and drained

3 cups roasted vegetable broth

1 bay laurel

1 thyme sprig, chopped

1 rosemary sprig, chopped

3 tablespoons olive oil

1 large onion, chopped

2 celery stalks, chopped

2 carrots, chopped

2 bell peppers, seeded and chopped

1 green chili pepper, seeded and chopped

2 garlic cloves, minced

Sea salt and ground black pepper, to taste

1 teaspoon cayenne pepper

1 teaspoon paprika

Directions

In a saucepan, bring the Anasazi beans and broth to a boil. Once boiling, turn the heat to a simmer. Add in the bay laurel, thyme and rosemary; let it cook for about 50 minutes or until tender.

Meanwhile, in a heavy-bottomed pot, heat the olive oil over medium-high heat. Now, sauté the onion, celery, carrots and peppers for about 4 minutes until tender.

Add in the garlic and continue to sauté for 30 seconds more or until aromatic.

Add the sautéed mixture to the cooked beans. Season with salt, black pepper, cayenne pepper and paprika.

Continue to simmer, stirring periodically, for 10 minutes more or until everything is cooked through. Bon appétit!

Easy and Hearty Shakshuka

(Ready in about 50 minutes | Servings 4)

Per serving : Calories: 324; Fat: 11.2g; Carbs: 42.2g; Protein: 15.8g

Ingredients

2 tablespoons olive oil

1 onion, chopped

2 bell peppers, chopped

1 poblano pepper, chopped

2 cloves garlic, minced

2 tomatoes, pureed

Sea salt and black pepper, to taste

1 teaspoon dried basil

1 teaspoon red pepper flakes

1 teaspoon paprika

2 bay leaves

1 cup chickpeas, soaked overnight, rinsed and drained

3 cups vegetable broth

2 tablespoons fresh cilantro, roughly chopped

Directions

Heat the olive oil in a saucepan over medium heat. Once hot, cook the onion, peppers and garlic for about 4 minutes, until tender and aromatic.

Add in the pureed tomato tomatoes, sea salt, black pepper, basil, red pepper, paprika and bay leaves.

Turn the heat to a simmer and add in the chickpeas and vegetable broth. Cook for 45 minutes or until tender.

Taste and adjust seasonings. Spoon your shakshuka into individual bowls and serve garnished with the fresh cilantro. Bon appétit!

Old-Fashioned Chili

(Ready in about 1 hour 30 minutes | Servings 4)

Per serving : Calories: 514; Fat: 16.4g; Carbs: 72g; Protein: 25.8g

Ingredients

3/4 pound red kidney beans, soaked overnight

2 tablespoons olive oil

1 onion, chopped

2 bell peppers, chopped

1 red chili pepper, chopped

2 ribs celery, chopped

2 cloves garlic, minced

2 bay leaves

1 teaspoon ground cumin

1 teaspoon thyme, chopped

1 teaspoon black peppercorns

20 ounces tomatoes, crushed

2 cups vegetable broth

1 teaspoon smoked paprika

Sea salt, to taste

2 tablespoons fresh cilantro, chopped

1 avocado, pitted, peeled and sliced

Directions

Cover the soaked beans with a fresh change of cold water and bring to a boil. Let it boil for about 10 minutes. Turn the heat to a simmer and continue to cook for 50 to 55 minutes or until tender.

In a heavy-bottomed pot, heat the olive oil over medium heat. Once hot, sauté the onion, bell pepper and celery.

Sauté the garlic, bay leaves, ground cumin, thyme and black peppercorns for about 1 minute or so.

Add in the diced tomatoes, vegetable broth, paprika, salt and cooked beans. Let it simmer, stirring periodically, for 25 to 30 minutes or until cooked through.

Serve garnished with fresh cilantro and avocado. Bon appétit!

Easy Red Lentil Salad

(Ready in about 20 minutes + chilling time | Servings 3)

Per serving : Calories: 295; Fat: 18.8g; Carbs: 25.2g; Protein: 8.5g

Ingredients

1/2 cup red lentils, soaked overnight and drained

1 ½ cups water

1 sprig rosemary

1 bay leaf

1 cup grape tomatoes, halved

1 cucumber, thinly sliced

1 bell pepper, thinly sliced

1 clove garlic, minced

1 onion, thinly sliced

2 tablespoons fresh lime juice

4 tablespoons olive oil

Sea salt and ground black pepper, to taste

Directions

Add the red lentils, water, rosemary and bay leaf to a saucepan and bring to a boil over high heat. Then, turn the heat to a simmer and continue to cook for 20 minutes or until tender.

Place the lentils in a salad bowl and let them cool completely.

Add in the remaining ingredients and toss to combine well. Serve at room temperature or well-chilled.

Bon appétit!

www.ingramcontent.com/pod-product-compliance
Lightning Source LLC
Chambersburg PA
CBHW071818080526
44589CB00012B/842